The GonMad Cumbrian Dictionary & Phrase Book

~~~

Dan Gibson

NOT!
No Original Thought

Praise for The GonMad Cumbrian Dictionary (online edition)

"The Inuit may have a hundred different words for snow, but the Cumbrians have a thousand ways to tell you about jumping over gates. While Cumbrian still continues to be snubbed by the likes of the Altavista translator, and it's still nearly impossible to find a decent tutor, at least one site is keeping the flame alive. Now, thanks to [the site's] courage and perseverance, you too can learn the appropriate way to tell someone that you jumped over a gate, are too tired to jump over gates, that you stole a gate, or that the next person who jumps over a gate is going to get slapped."

-Yahoo! Internet Life, Sept 2001.

"I was overjoyed to find your wonderful website..."

- Sue W

"A've found the Cumbrianator. Fabulous, eh!...this yan is jus' ower barie ter miss, eh!"

- Steve U

"I just wanted to say how pleased I am to be able to consult the Cumbrian dialect dictionary which is most useful."

- Tony J

"...wanted to let you know as an exiled Cumbrian I haven't laughed so much in ages!"

- Sue S

"Almost like being back there... Thanks for a great site, and the best laugh I've had in ages!"

- Alex B

"... this is the most brilliant thing I've seen for a long time. It has given our office hours of laughter, (I was in tears)"

- Stephen H

"I just want to say that I think it's is absolutely brilliant."

-Rob R

"I was totally amused by your cumbrian dictionary.
I was wondering if this had been put into a mini book form, as I would really like to buy it for a friend.
If you could please reply I would be very grateful, or if you know of any other cumbrian dialect books that are equally as funny."

-Kathleen B

The GonMad
Cumbrian
Dictionary
& Phrase Book

Published by No Original Thought

First Edition

First published in print December 2012

ISBN-13: 978-1481095303
ISBN-10: 1481095307

www.NoOriginalThought.com/cumbriandictionary

Also available as an eBook

The GonMad
Cumbrian Dictionary
& Phrase Book

For Kate,

for my Grandad

and for

Cumbrians and Cumbrian Ex-pats everywhere.

Contents

Introduction

Welcome to the first printed (and eBook) edition of the GonMad Cumbrian Dictionary.

This dictionary began life in 1997 as a tongue-in-cheek, online project to gather and preserve the slang of my youth growing up in Cumbria.

That means that the GonMad Cumbrian Dictionary website is older than both Facebook (by about seven years), YouTube (by about eight years) and Twitter (by about 9 years). Right now it has, therefore, been online longer than Facebook and YouTube combined. The Dictionary was born the same year as BBC.co.uk and is actually one year older than Google.com!

I'd like to consider those websites the younger cousins of this dictionary in the sense that we were all online pioneers (The GonMad Cumbrian Dictionary being the world's first website to include the words *gattered*, *kaleyed* and *arrished* on the same page – now if that's not pioneering I don't know what is). The aforementioned sites may have become a bit more successful a bit more quickly, but the dictionary is pretty popular too and has been featured on BBC Radio and in print and online reviews around the world.

Like a lot of good ideas, and many more bad ones, the Cumbrian Dictionary idea was born in a pub – this one a

I

pub down south. Over a pint with a Cumbrian friend we began reminiscing. It was interesting to find the differences between his West Cumbrian recollections and my East Cumbrian memories and so I began to build a list. What you now have in your hand(s) is the latest version of that list.

Exclusivity and Origination

It should be pointed out that I am claiming neither exclusivity nor origination of these words and phrases for Cumbria. Many of these words are shared with other dialects - Scots, Geordie and Yorkshire in particular - and many have been borrowed from places as far away as India and Australia with a lot of words seeming to have Scandinavian, Norse or Viking roots. I also shamelessly mix old words that may have a history in the old Cumbric language with more contemporary slang. In some cases derivation and etymology is mentioned. Mostly it is simply ignored – that kind of thing would be the subject of a far more serious and scholarly tome than this.

Neither do I claim any authority or special knowledge about Cumbrian. My only qualification for compiling this dictionary is that I spent the first 20-odd years of my life in Cumbria. When I left and ended up living down south, the only person who could really understand what I was talking about was that same West Cumbrian friend from the pub.

Offline and Online

For this printed edition the dictionary has been split into a traditional dictionary and a short phrase book - though some phrases remain in the dictionary as they seem to fit there better. Also included are some Cumbrian translations of short, famous texts for your amusement.

The GonMad Cumbrian Dictionary can still be found online at http://www.GonMad.co.uk and you can still submit new words that may be included in a future, updated edition.

In addition to the dictionary, our automated English to Cumbrian translator is also available online. Inspired by Douglas Adams' 'Babel-fish' from his 'Hitch Hikers...' books, this 'Cumbrianator' can be found at http://www.BabelSheep.com.

A note to parents

The dictionary and translator were always intended to be tongue-in-cheek and to be taken 'with a pretty large pinch of salt'.

As with any dictionary, there are some words and phrases that may not be exactly politically correct or particularly polite. In other words, you may not want your kids repeating everything you find within these pages. Let's not forget, though, that feeling of childhood naughtiness when sneaking a look at a rude word in the dictionary in the school library. For that reason - and because sometimes simply remembering those words is just funny - some of the less nice words are included but with definitions that hopefully obscure their meaning for those who would otherwise be unaware.

Back to reality

The web based edition of this dictionary invites visitors to submit any words that I have missed or forgotten. I am therefore indebted to many, many people who over the years have reminded me of words that have, almost without exception, raised a smile or chuckle.

Although many of the words included here have been submitted by those visitors to the online version of the dictionary, any errors are mine.

There were a number of words submitted numerous times by different people that I was not previously aware of. In these cases I have attempted to aggregate the definitions provided to give a generic meaning. Again, any errors are mine.

Please remember, though, that although the words and phrases herein are genuine words and phrases in use in and around Cumbria, the primary intention here is to amuse. That and to maybe even to trigger some nostalgia in those of you who, like myself, have had to leave the 'arl-lass-land'.

Dan Gibson, August 2012

THE GAMES OF XV CUMBRIAD

FER BAIRDENS

Knock 'n' Nash
Hikey Dikey

FER ARL UNS

Yat Lowpin
Gurnin'

GRAND FINAL EVENT

CHESS
Bairdens Vs Arluns

YAM MED SCORDY & SCRAN
SERVED ALL DAY

Dictionary

Cumbrian – English

A note on spelling:
The spelling of many Cumbrian words not only depends on where in the county you are, but on who you ask. Written Cumbrian varies widely, and so the spellings here are formed mostly phonetically. There are likely to be words where the spelling here is contentious, but one form had to be selected, and the decision became an arbitrary one. You'll still get the gist of things anyway.

A note on pronunciation:
This dictionary takes a phonetic approach to its pronunciation guide rather than the scheme of hieroglyphics more traditionally used. Say what you see and you won't go far wrong.

Note: In Cumbrian, unlike in Yorkshire dialect, a *t'* is a silent *t*. It is a sign of an amateur to pronounce the *t* and may indicate an interloper.

~A~

aas

> 1.*(verb.* arz*)* **I am**. From the verb to be. e.g. **Aas** ganna lowp awer yon yat = I am going to jump over that gate.
>
> *See also **arm**.*

ackers

> 1.*(noun.* akkurz*)* **money**. e.g. Aas out of **ackers** coz I was out last night = My cash flow situation has taken a turn for the worse due to my afterhours activities of last night.

afower

> 1.*(prep, conj, adj.* affawer*)* **before**. e.g. Av sin this yan **afower** = I believe I have seen this one before.

ah

> 1.*(pronoun.* ar*)* **I**. The first person singular.

any road

> 1.*(adv.* enee rohd*)* **anyway, anyhow**. e.g. Thoo'll tek nee notice **any road**! = You won't take any notice anyway.

arm

> 1.*(verb.* arm*)* **I am**, from the verb **to be**. e.g. **Arm** gam yam, this is radge = I am going home as I am not enjoying this much.

arl

> 1.*(adj.* arl*)* **old**. e.g. Deek at yon **arl** gadgee = Look at that old gentleman.
>
> 2.*(verb.* arl*)* **I will**. e.g. **Arl** dee it = I do. (As heard in Cumbrian wedding vows)
>
> 3.*(determiner, pronoun, adverb.* arl*)* **all**.

arl feller

> 1.*(noun.* arl fellur*)* **father.** e.g. Me **arl fellar** int flait a yoower **arl feller** = My father is not frightened of your father.

arl lass

> 1.*(noun.* arl lass*)* **mother.** e.g. Me **arl lass** int flait a yoower arl feller = My mother is not frightened of your father.

arrished

> 1.*(adj, verb.* arrisht*)* **motivated**, or **bothered**. e.g. I can't be **arrished** lowping awer t'yat today = I do not have the motivation required to perform gate jumping today.

> *(Note: No conjugation. Always used in the negative. No one can ever be arrished, regardless of whether they are first, second or third person...)*

asthoowivver

> 1.*(phrase.* ast-thoo-ivva*)* **Have you ever?** Uttered in incredulity. e.g. **Asthoowivver** met sec a grand feller? = A finer fellow you never shall meet.

away

> 1.*(verb.* a-way*)* **come on**, **hurry up**. e.g. **Away**, wiz ready ter gan. = Come on, we are ready to leave.

away chess

> 1.*(verb.* away chess*)* **go away**. e.g. **Away chess**, pal! = Would one mind please going away?

> 2.*(phrase.* away chess*)* **I don't believe you**. e.g. **Away chess**, pal! = I'm sorry but I just don't believe you.

awer

1.*(prep, adv.* awur*)* **over**. e.g. Lowp **awer** t'yat = Jump over the gate.

2.*(adv.* awur*)* **too**. e.g. I was jipped, two quid's **awer** dear furra pint = I was over charged, two pounds is rather expensive for a pint of beer.

awer theeyur

1.*(adj.* awur thee-ur*)* **at some distance**. e.g. Deeks yon **awer theeyur** = Look at that in the distance.

aye

1.*(excl.* ahyee*)* **yes**. Probably the most widespread slang word in the English language.

~B~

backend

>   1.*(noun.* bakkend*)* **end of the year, autumn/winter**. e.g. Cumt' **backend** o'the year thull be nee mare yat lowpin' = The gate jumping season is normaly over by the time the winter comes.

badly

>   1.*(adj.* badlee*)* **ill, poorly**. e.g. Aas nut comin' inter wuk t'day, aas **badly** = I shan't be attending my place of work this day as I am unwell.

bairden

>   1.*(noun.* behrdun*)* **child**, **offspring**. e.g. Hoost **bairdens** fettle? = How are the kids?

>   *Probably of Viking origin.*

bairn

>   1.*(noun.* behrn*)* See ***bairden***.

bait

>   1.*(noun.* bayt*)* **food**, particularly **packed lunch**. e.g. Am just mekkin me **bait**. = I am just packing these sandwiches, that I know'll be rancid by lunch time, and this banana, and this chocolate biscuit, and this munch bunch strawberry flavoured yoghurt in this old margarine/ice cream tub to take to work/school with me to provide sustenance during my lunch break.

bar

>   1.*(noun.* bar*)* **pound sterling**. e.g. Can yer len us two **bar**? = Would you be so kind as to loan me two English pounds?

>   *See also **pun**.*

barie

1.*(adj.* bar-ree*)* **good**. e.g. Ar like yat lowpin, it's **barie** = I like to jump over gates, it is good fun.

Often used in conjunction with the southern/London slang 'cushty' giving 'cushty barie' meaning very good.

beck

1.*(noun.* bek*)* **stream**. e.g. If yer cannut fin a yat ter lowp, yer can all'ers lowp tha **beck** = Streams make a suitable alternative if a gate cannot be found to jump.

bewer

1.*(noun.* byoowur*)* **girl/girlfriend**. e.g. Where's yer **bewer** at? = Could one tell me where one's young lady friend may be at this time.

birra

1.*(noun.* birrur*)* **bit of, piece of**. e.g. 'e's in a **birra** bother = He finds himself in a bit of trouble.

Black Eye Friday

1.*(noun.* blackiy frydur*)* **The last Friday before Christmas**. Not for the faint hearted.

blat

1.*(noun.* blat*)* **a go**, **a turn**. e.g. Giz a **blat** on yer bike, chore. = May I have a go on your bicycle, young man?

blether

1.*(verb.* blethur*)* **to talk unrelentingly**. e.g. Whits arl this **blethering**? = Why do you choose to talk so much?

bog

1.*(noun.* bog*)* **toilet**, **restroom**, **washroom**, **W.C.** e.g. I need the **bog** = I wish to visit the powder room / little boys room.

bonce

1.*(noun.* bons*)* **head.** e.g. On me **bonce**, chore = On my head, my son.

Border Crack and Deekabout

1.*(noun.* bordurcrakkundeeykabowt*)* **"Border News and Lookaround"**. Border TV's evening news magazine programme, known locally as the 'deekabout' (look around) as it looks at what is happening around the region. Literally translates as 'Border news and look around'.

So 'phenomenal' was the success of this week-daily broadcast, that wherever you went in Cumbria, the name and face of the late, great Eric Wallace (reporter and frequent anchor on the show since the beginning) was known by everyone young and old.

bother

1.*(noun.* bothur*)* **trouble**, as in getting into trouble. e.g. Divn't git inter any **bother** = stay out of trouble.

2.*(noun.* bothur*)* **trouble**, as in it's no problem. e.g. Aye, It's nee **bother** = Yes, of course, it's no problem.

3.*(verb.* bothur*)* **trouble**. e.g. Gan **bother** yer boyo, yer arl feller's awer thrang = Go trouble your brother, your father is too busy.

bowk

1.*(verb.* bowk*)* **to vomit**. e.g. I had a few pints last night, but it must have been a bad pint that med us **bowk** = I did drink a little last night, but I think one of the drinks must have been out of condition as I vomitted.

(I **bowk**, you **bowk**, he **bowks**, they **bowk**).

Cumbrian clubs and pubs have been known to run 'Bowk and you're out' nights whereby a fixed entry fee is charged and all drinks are free – until you vomit and are ejected from the establishment.

*See also **chunder**.*

2.*(verb.* bowk*)* **to burp loudly**.

boyo

1.*(noun.* boy-oh*)* **brother**. e.g. Yer **boyo** can't 'arf lowp yats. = I do believe your brother is rather good at jumping over gates.

Not to be confused with the Welsh 'boyo' which has a less specific meaning.

brant

1.*(adj.* brant*)* **steep**. e.g. Ah cowped awer nashin doon yon fell cuz it's gay **brant** = As I ran down that lakeland hill I took a tumble as it is rather steep.

brat

1.*(noun.* brat*)* **apron** or **pinny**.

2.*(noun.* brat*)* **unruly child** or just a **child** in general.

bratful o' mowdies

1.*(phrase.* bratfull oh mowdeez*)* **apronful of moles**. e.g. Bewer's gut bratful o mowdies = The lady is rather plump.

bray

1.*(verb.* bray*)* **to hit** or **strike**. e.g. 'is father'll **bray** 'im when he gits yam = His father shall be so displeased on his return home that he may discipline him physically.

*(I **bray**, you **bray**, he **brays**, they **brayed**).*

brossen

1.*(adj.* brossun*)* **being full of food**. e.g. A wafer thin mint? No ta, aas **brossen** = I have no space for even a wafer thin mint, I'm close to bursting.

bust

1.*(verb.* bust*)* **to break**, or **damage**. e.g. Y'll **bust** yon yat if ya keep lowpin awer it = You stand the chance of damaging that gate if you persist with jumping over it.

*(I **bust**, you **bust**, he **busts**, it **busts**).*

2.*(adj.* bust*)* **broken**. e.g. Yon yat's **bust** = That gate is broken.

buthder

1.*(noun.* buthdur*)* **birthday**. e.g. It wuz 'is **buthder**, gittin' gattered's nowt ter gan radge awer = One shouldn't object to him enjoying a couple of sherries once a year.

butty

1.*(noun.* buttee*)* **sandwich**. e.g. Arv a **butty** in me bate fer me dinner ivry day, that an' a flask o' scordy = One is wont to partake in a sandwich and a nice cup of tea for one's lunch most days.

~C~

cailo

> 1.*(noun.* kiylow*)* **money**. e.g. I've got nee **cailo** left coz I was out last night = My cash flow situation has taken a turn for the worse due to my afterhours activities of last night.
>
> *See also **lowie**.*

carlin

> 1.*(noun.* karlin*)* **chick pea**. The perfect ammunition for a pea-shooter.

chaff

> 1.*(verb.* chaff*)* **to steal**. e.g. I **chaffed** it = I stole it.
>
> *(I **chaff**, you **chaff**, she **chaffs**, they **chaffed**).*
>
> *See also **chore**.*

charver

1.*(noun.* charver*)* **boy**, or **lad**. e.g. Deek at that **charver** lowpin awer t'yat = Look at that boy jumping over the gate.

> In some areas of the UK charver has taken on a pejorative sense — this is not strictly the case in Cumbria where it is a far more general term.

chebble

1.*(noun.* chebbul*)* **table**. e.g. Arl git some scran on **chebble** if thees hungry = I'll rustle up something to eat if you like.

chess

1.*(noun.* chess*)* A game enjoyed by Cumbrians from around early walking years through to mid-to-late teens — though some crawling infants have also been known to make a good go of it. Forget your Kasparovs and your Deep Blues, the Cumbrian version of Chess is an outdoor sport (usually), involving being chased from either a park by the 'Parky' (Park keeper) or from a building site by the 'Watchy' (Watchman). Chess was often the culmination of a game of Hikey Dikey, or Knock-n-Nash.

> See also **Hikey Dikey** and **Knock-n-Nash**.

chitta

1.*(adj.* chittur*)* **fit and healthy**, **well**. e.g. Aas **chitta** like owt = I'm very well, couldn't be better.

chore

1.*(verb.* chor*)* **to steel**, or **pinch**. e.g. I **chored** a yat on Sat'day when I was gattered = I stole a gate on Saturday when I was under the influence of alcohol.

> (I **chore**, you **chore**, he is a **chorer**, it is **chored**).

> See also **chaff**.

2.*(noun.* chor*)* **stolen item**. e.g. That's a good **chore** = That was a good item to steel.

*See also **choredy**.*

3.*(noun.* chor*)* **boy**, or **lad**. Short for charver, esp. younger boys. e.g. Deek at that la'l **chor** lowpin awer t'yat = Look at that younger boy jumping over the gate.

choredy

1.*(noun.* chordy*)* **stolen items**. e.g. He's got loadsa **choredy** in his arl feller's shed = He has a considerable amount of stolen property in his father's wooden outbuilding.

chowy

1.*(noun.* chowwee*)* **love bite**. e.g. Have yer sin the **chowy** his bewer give him? = Have you happened to notice the red mark on his neck administered by his lady friend?

chuddy

1.*(noun.* chuddee*)* **chewing gum**. e.g. Giz a birra **chuddy** = Would you mind if I had a piece of your chewing gum, please?

chull

1.*(vulg. noun.* chull*)* **male member**, not of a club!

*See also **cordy**.*

chunder

1.*(verb.* chundur*)* **to vomit**. e.g. I 'ad see much peeve I **chundered** = I consumed such an excess of alcohol I projectile vomitted.

(I chunder, you chunder, he's chundering, what a party).

*See also **bowk**.*

chunter

1.*(verb.* chuntur*)* **to talk nonsense or otherwise incoherently**. e.g. Whits the **chuntering** about? = Do tell about what it is you are talking.

claggy

1.*(adj.* klaggee*)* **dirty**, **mucky.** e.g. His shoes were arl **claggy** after the yat lowpin competition = His shoes were very dirty after the gate jumping competition.

*See also **clarty***

clart

1.*(noun.* klart*)* **cosmetic make-up**. e.g. Yer look like a clown wearin' arl that **clart** = I think you may have over done the lippy and blusher, darling.

clarty

1.*(adj.* klartee*)* **dirty**, **mucky** particularly in a sticky toffee on your hands kind of way. Kids get clarty when they eat candy floss or when they eat ice cream.

*See also **claggy***

clegg

1.*(noun.* klegg*)* **horsefly**. e.g. Yon **clegg** just bit uz on the neb. = That horsefly just bit me on the nose.

clemmies

1.*(plural noun.* klemmeez*)* half brick sized **stones**, or **rocks**. e.g. They were gan radge an' started hoyin' **clemmies** at us, like eh! = They seemed a little perturbed and began to launch projectiles in our direction.

Can also be used to refer to testicles.

cleppets

> 1.*(plural noun.* kleppurtz*)* **testicles**. e.g. Ah knack'd me **cleppets** when ah landed on yon yat = I caused some injury to my under-carriage as I landed incorrectly when jumping the gate.

clicked

> 1.*(verb.* klikt*)* **caught**. e.g. Ah gut **clicked** playin' hikey dikey = I got caught jumping the neighbourhood's hedges.

clout

> 1.*(verb.* klowt*)* **to hit**, or **slap**, or **punch**. e.g. If thee keeps on about lowpin awer yats, arl **clout** ya = I you persist in talking about the practice of gate jumping, I will be forced to slap you.

> *(I **clout**, you **clout**, he got **clouted**, she **clouts**).*

cod-eye

> 1.*(adj.* koddiy*)* **not straight**, or **at an angle**. e.g Yon yat looks bust, it's all **cod-eye** = That gate looks as though it may have been damaged as it is not hanging quite true.

> *See also **jye**.*

coddie

> 1.*(noun.* koddee*)* **stone**, or **pebble**. e.g. A good way of startin' a gem o' chess is to chuck a **coddie** at an old gadgee's window = One finds that an oft successful way of attracting someone into the street to pursue one is to project small pieces of rock material at their fenestrations.

come by

> 1.*(phrase.* kum by*)* **stand aside**. e.g. **Come by**, giz a glem? = Stand aside in order that I may see what it is upon which you are gazing.

> *From the traditional sheep dog command.*

15

cous

1.*(noun.* kuz*)* **friend**, or **mate**. e.g. Areet, **cous**? = Hello my friend.

From cousin.

cop hod

1.*(phrase.* koppod*)* **take hold**. e.g. **Cop hod** o' yon while ar lowps awer t'yat then scop it awer till us. = Would you please take hold of this for me while I jump over this here gate. Then if you'd be so kind as to throw it over to me.

coppy

1.*(noun.* koppee*)* **small stool, milking stool**. e.g. A **coppy** needs three legs ur it'll cowp awer = Three legs are required for a stable stool.

cordy

1.*(vulg. noun.* kordee*)* another **male member**, also not of a club!

*See also **chull**.*

cowie

1.*(pronoun.* kow-wee*)* **a thing**. e.g. Deek at yon **cowie** = Look at that thing.

*An especially good word for combining with other Cumbrian words. e.g. **Lowie cowie** = cash point/ATM.*

Pronounced cower (cow-wur) in some areas, which is not so good for combining with lowie as it sounds a bit radge, eh.

*See also **Lowie Cowie**.*

cowies

1.*(plural noun.* kow-weez*)* **things**. e.g. Deek at yon **cowies** = Look at those things.

2.*(noun.* kow-weez*)* **Up-turned bicycle handle bars**. e.g. Deek at yon **cowies** = Look at those up-turned bicycle handle bars, they're great !

cowp

1.*(verb.* kowp*)* **fall**. e.g. **Cowp** awer = fall over.

*(I **cowp** awer, you **cowped** awer, she is **cowping** awer, we are all **cowpers** awer).*

crack

1.*(noun.* krak*)* **gossip**, or **news**. e.g. 'Ave ye heard the **crack**? Thuz gunna be a yat lowping competition on Satdur. = Have you heard the news? A gate jumping competition is to be held this coming Saturday.

*See also **Border Crack and Deekabout***

crag

1.*(noun.* krag*)* **rock face** or **rocky outcrop**. e.g. Helm Crag to the north of Grassmere with the famous 'Lion and the Lamb' at its summit.

cuddy

1.*(noun.* kuddee*)* **donkey**. e.g. 'Ave yer ivver sin a **cuddy** lowp a yat? = Have you, perchance, observed a donkey jump over a gate?

Note: Cuddy is often apparently mistakenly translated to cow. I am assured by a number of reliable sources, however, that Donkey is the correct translation. Somehow, this has not stopped phrases such as 'cuddy splatter' evolving!

cuddy splatter

1.*(phrase.* cuddee splattur*)* **cow pat**, **bovine excrement**. This phrase is a corruption of the real meaning of cuddy which is actually a donkey!

*See also **cuddy**.*

 17

cuddy wifted

1.*(adj.* kuddee wiftid*)* **inept**, **cack handed**. e.g. E's **cuddy wifted** that gadgee, deeks the maff 'es med o' yon. = That gentleman is not really suited to that task.

2.*(adj.* kuddee wiftid*)* **left handed**.

cut

1.*(noun.* kut*)* **passageway**, **lane** esp. between streets.

cuvvin

1.*(noun.* kuvvin*)* **littorina littorea**. e.g. Aas 'avin **cuvvins** fur me tea.

~D~

deek

> 1.*(verb.* deek*)* **to look**. e.g. **Deek** at yon yat = look at that gate.
>
> > *(I **deek**, you **deek**, he **deeks**, it is **deeking**).*

deekabout

> 1.*(verb.* deeykabowt*)* **to look around**. e.g. Aas gan up street ter **deekabout** = I am going into the city center shopping area to look around.
>
> > *(I **deekabout**, you **deekabout**, he **deeksabout**, it is **deekingabout**).*
>
> 2.*(noun.* deekabowt*)* **a look around**. e.g. Aas gan up street furra **deekabout** = I am going into the city center shopping area for a look around.
>
> > *See also **Border Crack and Deekabout***

deeks

> 1.*(noun.* deeks*)* **A viewing**, or **a look at**. e.g. Giz a **deeks** at yon yat = Please, would you mind if I had a look at that gate ?
>
> > *See also **deek** and **glem**.*

dial

> 1.*(noun.* diyal*)* **face**. e.g. Do you want a smack in the **dial** = Would you like me to hit you in the general area of your face ?

dido

1.*(noun.* diydo*)* **gypsy**, **potter**, **traveller or tinker**. Not necessarily used as an offensive term, but possibly perceived as such. It is a general term for a gypsy; someone who maybe deals in 'rag'n'bone' and scrap; or someone who goes door to door mending things, especially metalwork and ironmongery.

dike

1.*(noun.* diyk*)* **hedge**. e.g. If yur cannut fin a yat ter lowp, lowp a **dike**. = If you are having trouble locating a suitable gate for your jumping pleasure, perhaps you would be more successful looking for a hedgerow to jump.

> *Not to be confused with dyke which retains the traditional English meaning of ditch or watercourse.*

dinner

1.*(noun.* dinnur*)* **the midday meal**. Dinner is served at midday, not in the evening. Tea is served in the evening. It's easy to remember which is which as dinner can be served by 'dinner ladies'.

dish

1.*(noun.* dish*)* **face**. e.g. Nice legs, shame about the **dish** = That young woman has very nice legs, it is a shame that her facial features let her overall appearance down somewhat.

divn't

1.*(negative verb.* divvunt*)* **don't**, **do not**. e.g. **Divn't** lowp awer t'yat. = Don't jump over the gate.

divvy

1.*(noun.* divvee*)* **idiot**. e.g. Divn't dee that yer **divvy**! = Don't do that you idiot.

> *Can be shortened to **div**.*

do / doo

> 1.*(noun.* doo*)* **party, social occasion**. e.g. They're 'avin' a **doo** fur is old man's buthder = They are celebrating his father's birthday with a party.

> 2.*(noun.* doo*)* **hairstyle**. e.g. She got a new **do** fur the do = she has had her hair cut and styled especially for the party.

donnat

> 1.*(noun.* donnert*)* **idiot**, **fool**. e.g. Give awer yer **donnat**, away chess = I'm afraid I don't agree with your opinion, be off with you.

dook

> 1.*(noun.* dook*)* **a swim**. e.g. As gan furra **dook** = I'm going for a swim.

dookers

> 1.*(pl. noun.* dookerz*)* **swimming trunks**, '**Speedos**® '. Not often called for in Cumbria. In best English tradition, Cumbrians go to the beach fully clothed. With sweaters on. And coats. Scarves as well, usually.

doss

> 1.*(verb.* doss*)* **to play**. e.g. Arm only **dossin**' = I'm only playing.

> *(I **doss**, I was **dossin'**, I have **dossed**, he **dosses**).*

> 2.*(noun.* doss*)* **a trivial matter**, **a joke** or a **non-serious activity**. e.g. I only did it furra **doss** = I only did it for a laugh.

dow

> 1.*(pronoun.* dahw*)* **a portion**, esp. **the last of something**. The last cigarette, or the last few mouthfuls of a drink. e.g. Save us a **dow** = Would you be so kind as to save me the last mouthful of your tasty beverage?

21

dyur

1.*(verb.* dyur*)* **to suffice**. Literally 'to do you'.
e.g.
Richard III: My kingdom for a horse.
Voice from the gods: Wud a cuddy nut **dyur**? = A horse is rather an extravagant request, would a donkey suffice?

~E~

effort

1.*(noun.* effort*)* **thing**. Generally derogatory, e.g. Deek at that **effort**, eh! = Look at that thing, it's not very good is it?

eh

1.*(suffix.* ay*)* **Do you agree**, or **you see**. A general suffix, e.g. Lowpin' awer la'l yats is easier than big yans, **eh** ? = Jumping over small gates is easier than big ones, do you agree ?

~F~

farmer's hankey

> 1.*(phrase.* farmurs 'ankee*)* See potter's fling.

fash

> 1.*(verb.* fash*)* **to bother**, **to trouble**. Usually used in the negative. e.g. Divn't **fash** thissen = don't trouble yourself.

fatheed

> 1.*(noun.* fatteed*)* **rash** and/or **accident prone person**. Usually used in the negative. e.g. Watcher deeing lyin' in the clart be t'yat, yer **fatheed** = One should be more careful when jumping over gates, save, perchance, you'll find yourself taking a tumble.

feckless

> 1.*(adj.* fek-less*)* **useless**, **of no worth**. e.g. That **feckless** fatheed couldn't even lowp awer a small yat = That unfortunate person was unable to jump over a small gate.

fell

> 1.*(noun.* fell*)* **lakeland hill**. e.g. If the can see clouds awer yon **fells** it's ganna rain, if the cannut it's arlriddy rainin' = If you can see clouds over those hills then it is going to rain, if you can't see them then it's already raining.

feller

> 1.*(noun.* fellur*)* **man**. e.g Yon **feller** can't 'alf lowp yats = That gentleman over there is rather proficient at gate jumping.

fettle

1.*(noun.* fettul*)* **condition**, **health**. e.g. After Sat'da neets gatterin at t'oldhall, ah waz nut a grand **fettle** = After Saturday night's entertainments in Egremont, I didn't feel too well.

2.*(verb.* fettul*)* **to fix**, **to repair.** e.g. That'll **fettle** it. = I think that may fix it.

*(I am **fettlin** it, I was **fettlin** it, I have **fettled** it, He **fettles** stuff.)*

fizzog

1.*(noun.* fizz-ogg*)* **face**. e.g. 'e cowped awer an landed smack on his **fizzog**. = He fell over and landed on his face.

flait / flaiten

1.*(adj.* flayt/faytun*)* **frightened**. e.g. A wuz gay **flaiten** = I was very frightened. Aas nut **flait** o' thew, pal = I'm not scared of you, good sir.

flivvas

1.*(noun.* flivvers*)* **limpets**. Those aquatic gastropod mollusks, usually belonging to the clade Patellogastropoda and having a simple, non-coiled shell.

flukey

1.*(adj.* flookee*)* **lucky**. e.g. The Parky nivver clicked 'im, 'e's **flukey** like that! = He evaded capture by the park warden as ever.

*See also **spawney** and **jousey**.*

foily

1.*(adj.* foylee*)* **smelly**, **prone to breaking wind**. e.g. He's been eatin cabbage again, and 'e int half **foily** = Due to the fact that he has eaten cabbage, it is advised that you give him a wide birth for olfactory reasons.

force

> 1.*(noun.* fors*)* **waterfall**. e.g. Aira Force to the north of Ulswater.
>
> *From the old Norse* fors*.*

frey

> 1.*(prep.* fray*)* **from**, e.g. As **frey** Wukitun = I hail from the town of Workington.

frizzened

> 1.*(adj.* frizzund*)* **burned**. e.g. **Frizzened** bacon's best in a butty = Burned bacon is the best for sandwiches.

fyace

> 1.*(noun.* fee-yass*)* **face**. e.g. 'e 'ad a **fyace** like a babby's slapped backside = He had his sulky face on.
>
> *See also* **dial** *and* **mask***.*

~G~

gadgee

1.*(noun.* gadjee*)* **man**, or **bloke**. e.g. **Gadgees** can still lowp yats like the la'l chores can = Gate jumping does not seperate the men from the boys.

gammy

1.*(adj.* gammeey*)* **rotten**, **rancid**, **festering.** e.g. He's gashed his leg an' its arl gone **gammy**. = He has wonded his leg, and it appears to have become infected.

gallusses

1.*(plural noun.* gallussiz*)* **braces** (or **suspenders** to any American readers). What hods yer kecks up.

gan

1.*(verb.* gan*)* **to go**. e.g. Aas **gan** yam to lowp awer t'yat = I am going home to jump over the gate.

*(I am **gan**, I was **gannin**, I have **gone**, He **gars**, She's a bit of a **ganner**.)*

gander

> 1.*(noun.* gandur*)* **a look**. e.g. Giz a **gander** at yon = Could one please take a look at that.

ganzee / ganzy

> 1.*(noun.* gan-zee*)* **jacket** or **jumper.** e.g. Deeks at yon's smart new **ganzee**. = Look at that gentleman's new jacket, it's very nice, isn't it?

gattered

> 1.*(adj.* gattud*)* **drunk**. e.g. I wuz seh **gattered** at'oldhall I chucked my guts arl t'way yam. = I was so inebtriated at the Old Hall, I experienced vomitting for most of my journey returning to my dwelling place.

gay

> 1.*(adv, adj.* gay*)* **very**, e.g. It's **gay** cold out at the minute. = Brrrr, it's rather chilly, what?

gen

> 1.*(noun.* jen*)* **gossip**, **information**. e.g. 'ave yur got any **gen** furrus ? = Do you have any information which may be of interest to me ?

gert

> 1.*(adj.* gurt*)* **big**. e.g. Yon's a **gert** biggun. = That's a big one.

ghyll

> 1.*(noun.* gill*)* **stream** / **waterfall** running down a hill in a rocky crack or mini ravine.

gia

> 1.*(noun.* jee-ah*)* **posterior**. e.g. 'e landed on 'is **gia** = He landed on his bottom.

gimmer

1.*(noun.* gimmurr*)* **young female sheep**. Contrary to the belief of some, this does not make the gimmer automatically eligible for marriage.

giz

1.*(verb.* gizz*)* **give me**. e.g. **Giz** a glem at yon = Would you mind if I took a look at that, please.

Note: Giz is a contraction of 'Give us'. 'Us' in this case, as is often the case in Cumbrian, is the first person singular!

gizzasec

1.*(phrase.* gizz-ah-seck*)* **wait a moment**. e.g. **Gizzasec**, am just gonna lowp yon yat = Wait one moment if you would, I wish to jump over that gate.

glabbie

1.*(noun.* glabbee*)* **marble**. The small round glass object so coveted by kids in times gone by.

glem

1.*(noun.* glem*)* **a look**. e.g. giz a **glem** at that picture of the l'arl chore lowpin awer the yat = let me see the picture you have of the young lad jumping over the gate.

See also ***deeks***.

glishy

1.*(adj.* glishee*)* **bright, shiny**.

gowk

1.*(noun.* gowk*)* **ugly bloke**. e.g. How does a **gowk** like that git a smart bewer like her? = Do you think that gentleman may be very rich?

29

grotch

> 1.*(verb.* grotsh*)* **to spit**. e.g. Ah wudden **grotch** on 'im if 'e wuz a'fire = I do not think much of that young man. (Literally "I wouldn't spit on him if he was on fire".)
>
> > *(I **grotch**, you **grotch**, he **grotches**, I **grotched**, look who's **grotching**)*
>
> 2.*(noun.* grotsh*)* **spit**. The product of 'grotching'.

grotts

> 1.*(noun.* grotts*)* **underpants**. e.g. Ah divn't wear any **grotts** when ah gan down t'oldhall cuz the motts in theeyur love it, like = I refrain from wearing undergarments when visiting the Old Hall, because it makes me more attractive to the women-folk.

gurn

> 1.*(verb.* gurn*)* **to pull an unattractive face**. Gurning is perhaps Cumbria's most famous export after sausage thanks to the annual Egremont Crab Fair at which the World Gurning Championships are held every year. Participants, often without teeth to enhance the look, will poke their head through a horse's bridle and gurn to win prizes and the adulation of spectators.

~H~

hesta

1.*(phrase.* hesturr*)* **Have you?** e.g. **Hesta** ivver sin a cuddy lowp a yat? = Has one perchance observed a donkey jump over a gate?

Hikey Dikey

1.*(noun.* iykey diykey*)* This game is the ultimate 'yat lowpin' practice. Enjoyed by Cumbrian kids since time began (or at least since we came down from the trees), it involves running across the gardens of adjoining houses (or huts or caves if it was shortly after we came down from the trees), and hurdling the fences, hedges, and gates encountered on the way. The aim of the game being to get through as many gardens as possible before being caught. If caught the game would often escalate into a game of Chess.

*See also **chess**.*

hod

1.*(verb.* hodd*)* **to hold**. e.g. **Hod** on a l'arl lok, arl be riddy in a bit = Have patience, my fellow, for I shall be with you presently.

hoor

1.*(noun.* hoo-ur*)* **lady of questionable repute**. e.g. She's nowt but a dirty **hoor** = It is possible that she may be prepared to enter into short term relations with a variety of persons with whome she may have had no previous acquaintance.

Probably derived from 'whore', but need not be practising for profit.

horney

>1.*(noun.* hor-nee*)* **policeman**. e.g. Sometimes whenyer git caught playin' hikey dikey, ole gadgees'll git the **'orneys** = It is possible that when caught playing 'hikey dikey' you may attract the attention of the law.

how

>1.*(noun.* hahw*)* **small hill**. Used only in place names such as Tarn Hows near Coniston.

howk

>1.*(verb.* hahwk*)* **to pull** or **dig something out**. e.g. He **howked** a big ole bogey oot 'is neb = he dug around in his nose and drew out a large piece of congealed mucus.

>*(I **howk**, you **howk**, he **howks**, I **howked**).*

hoy

>1.*(verb.* hoy*)* **to throw**. e.g. **Hoy** yon awer 'ere = Would you mind throwing that over to me, please.

>*(I **hoy**, you **hoy**, he **hoys**, I **hoyed**).*

hoy up

>1.*(verb.* hoy up*)* **to vomit**. e.g. Eatin' awer much taytee pot afore lowpin yats will mek yer **hoy up** = Over indulgence in meat and potatoe based casserole style dishes before indulging in gate jumping may lead to vomitus.

>*(I **hoy up**, you **hoy up**, he **hoys up**, I **hoyed up**).*

~J~

jam eater

1.*(noun.* jam eeter*)* **resident of Whitehaven/Workington**.
Offensive. Not to be used unless you fancy a 'pagga'

> *The story goes that the mines in Workington closed and all the Workintoners started working in the mines in Whitehaven. The Whitehaveners claim all the Workington miners came to work with jam sandwiches and the Workingtoners claim it was the Whitehaveners. It's now a term of abuse that both West Cumbrian towns use on each other especially at Whitehaven / Workington rugby derby matches.*

jewkle

1.*(noun.* djoowkel*)* **dog**. e.g. Tek **jewkle** furra walk, eh? = Would you mind taking our beloved canine companion out for his daily exercise?

jarmiz

1.*(noun.* djarmeez*)* **pyjamas**. e.g. Divn't lowp yats in yer **jarmiz**, yurl split 'em = Pyjamas are not suitable attire for gate jumping, they are prone to splitting.

jipped

1.*(verb.* jipt*)* to be **ripped off**, **conned**. e.g. Ah wuz **jipped**, two quid's awer dear furra pint = I was over charged, two pounds is rather expensive for a pint of beer.

jousey

1.*(adj.* jow-see*)* **lucky**. e.g. He was a bit **jousey** ter git awer yon yat = He was rather lucky to make it over that gate.

*See also **spawney** and **flukey**.*

jye

1.*(adj.* jiyee*)* **not straight**. e.g. Yon picture's a bit **jye**. = That picture needs to be straightened.

*See also **cod-eye**.*

~K~

KAYDIE

kaleyed

    1.*(adj.* kayl-iyd*)* **drunk**. e.g. I had see much last night ah wuz **kaleyed** = I drank a couple to many last night, and ended up more than a little tipsy.

kady / kaydie

    1.*(noun.* kay-dee*)* **hat**. e.g. Yer'll catcher death if ye gan oot widoot theez **kaydie** = it is advisable to wear one's hat when venturing out, else one is likely to become unwell.

kebbie

    1.*(noun.* kebbee*)* **stick** or **staff** often with a hooked head. e.g. Dee that again an arl clout yer wid me **kebbie** = If you persist in doing that I shall hit you with my stout staff.

kecks

    1.*(noun.* kecks*)* **trousers**. e.g. That la'l charver ripped his **kecks** lowpin' awer yonder yat = That young boy tore his breeches when he hurdled that gate over there.

ken

1.*(verb.* ken*)* **to know**. e.g. Dust the **ken** John Peel wi' 'is coat see grey = Do you know John Peel with his coat so grey.

Also in wide use in Scotland.

kessen

1.*(adj.* kessun*)* **prostrate**, **prone**, **recumbent.** e.g. A wuz **kessen** an 'ad ter be dragged up by me marras = After I fell on my back hurdling the gate, I had to be helped to my feet by my compadrés as I was unable to erect myself.

Knock-n-Nash

1.*(noun.* nocken nash*)* Another Cumbrian outdoor sport, this one played around the whole of the UK under different names (Ring and Run, etc). This game involves knocking on a house door and running away before the door can be answered. Advanced options include then hiding, and watching someone come to the door and be puzzled by the fact there is no-one there. Hours of fun can be had until you are caught on someone's doorstep, in which case honour dictates that you run anyway (making excuses to whoever answers the door is for sissies). Often the game will then develop into a nice game of Chess.

*See also **chess**.*

~L~

la'l

> 1.*(adj.* larl*)* **small**. e.g. Lowpin' awer **la'l** yats is easier than lowping' awer bigger yans = Jumping over small gates is easier than jumping over bigger ones.

laddo

> 1.*(noun.* laddow*)* **boy, man**. e.g. **Laddo** awer theeyur's gan radge = There is a gentleman over here who seems somewhat agitated.

ladge

> 1.*(verb.* ladj*)* **to shame** or **to be shamed**.

ladgeful

1.*(adj.* ladjfull*)* **embarrassing**. e.g. 'e wuz see bad at yat lowpin it wur **ladgeful** = He was so bad at jumping over gates, he was an embarrassment to us all.

Note: Ladgeful is/was also interchangeable with radge in some areas to mean rubbish, not very good, or unfair i.e. worthy of causing embarrassment.

lag

1.*(noun.* lagg*)* **urine**, **wee-wee.** e.g. aas ganna tek a **lag** = I am taking leave to micturate.

*See also **waz**.*

laik / lake

1.*(verb.* layk*)* **to play**.

Not to be confused with lake meaning a body of water. Technically there is only one lake in the English Lake District - all others are meres, waters or tarns - and any true Cumbrian should know which one that is.

lamp

1.*(verb.* lamp*)* **to hit**. Am gunna **lamp** 'im fur deekin at me bewer. = I shall hit the gentleman for glancing at my lady-friend.

*(I **lamp**, I have **lamped**, I am **lamping**, He **lamps**, She is a **lamper**.)*

lang

1.*(adj, adv.* lang*)* **long** e.g. 'ave yer bin waiting **lang**, lad? = Have you been waiting for a long time, young man?

Not just a pronunciation difference, lang is probably of Viking origin.

lashed

> 1.*(adj.* lasht*)* **drunk**. e.g. A wuz **lashed** Sat'der. = I was a little inebriated on Saturday.

lasso

> 1.*(noun.* lassow*)* **girl, woman**. e.g. That's nee laddo, it's a **lasso** we a tash.

lecky

> 1.*(noun.* lekky*)* **electricity**. New fangled thing that is being installed in some homes that makes light without fire.

like

> 1.*(phrase.* liyk*)* **You see!** A general suffix, e.g. I'm ganna lowp awer t'yat, **like** = I am going to jump over the gate, you see!

like, eh

> 1.(phrase. liyk-eh) The customary end of any sentence. Has no meaning itself but it can be used wherever a full-stop can be used making it more like punctuation, **like eh**.
>
> *Note that 'like, eh' should not be considered a sign of illiteracy in the way 'innit' is. It is more like the Brummie custom of repeating the verb at the end of every sentence, it is.*

lok

> 1.*(noun.* lokk*)* **non-specific quantity**. Used in conjunction with la'l or gay to give la'l **lok** = a small amount, and gay **lok** = a lot.

lonnin

> 1.*(noun.* lonnin*)* **lane, country road**. e.g. Ah last sin 'im on the back **lonnin** = I last saw him on the local country road that we all know locally as the 'back lonnin'.

39

lowie

> 1.*(noun.* la-weey*)* **money**. e.g. I've got nee **lowie** left coz I was out last night = My cash flow situation has taken a turn for the worse due to my after-hours activities of last night.
>
> > *See also **cailo**.*

lowie cowie

> 1.*(noun.* la-weey ca-wee*)* **cash point**, **ATM**. e.g. Arv gotta gan ter the **lowie cowie** coz I've gut nin left = My cash flow situation has taken a turn for the worse so I must make a withdrawal from the hole in the wall.

lowp

> 1.*(verb.* lowp*)* **jump**. e.g. **Lowp** awer t'yat = Jump over the gate.
>
> > *(I **lowp**, I have **lowped**, I am **lowping**, He **lowps**, She is a **lowper**.)*
>
> > *See also **Hikey Dikey**.*

lugs / lug holes

> 1.*(noun.* luggz / lug ohlz*)* **ears**. e.g. Deek at the **lugs** on that gowk, 'e looks like the World Cup.

~M~

maff

1.*(noun.* maff*)* **something that has been made a mess of**. e.g. That radgee's made a right **maff** of that = That unfortunately incapable person has not done that quite so well as I had hoped.

2.*(verb.* maff*)* **to make a mess of**. e.g. Don't **maff** it up ya radgee = Please don't make a mess of what it is you are about to do you unfortunately incapable person.

   *(I **maff**, you **maff**, he **maffs**, she **maffs**, we **maff**, yous **maff**, they **maff**, I have **maffed**, I will **maff**, I am a radgee)*

mannar

1.*(noun.* mannahr*)* **fat women/girl**. e.g. Deek at that **mannar** = That is a shame, I really feel sorry for that woman, she appears to have a serious weight problem, maybe it's glandular.

   This term seems to have sadly fallen out of use. It's origin may be the term 'mna' as found on the door of ladies toilets in so called 'Irish bars' around England. Maybe it's time for a comeback?

mare

1.*(pronoun.* mehr*)* **more**. e.g. Arl 'ave nee **mare** o'that, pal! = A shall take no more of that, sir!

marra

1.*(pronoun.* marra*)* **mate**. e.g. Y'arlreet **marra** ? = How are you, my friend ?

41

mask

> 1.*(noun.* mask*)* **face**.
>
> > See also ***dial*** *and **fyace**.*

me

> 1.*(possessive determiner.* mee*)* **my**. e.g. 'Ave yer sin **me** mam? = Have you seen my mother?
>
> 2.*(pronoun.* mee*)* **me**! e.g. **Me** an' me arl lass, an' me arl feller, an' me grandma = Me and my mam, and my dad, and my gran.

mell

> 1.*(noun.* mell*)* **large hammer, sledge hammer.** e.g. Ah smacked my thumb wid me **mell** = Oops! I seem to have hit my thumb with this large hammer.

methera

> 1.*(cardinal number.* methurra*)* **four**. The fourth number. Part of the old Cumbrian sheep counting scheme.
>
> > See phrase book.

mind

> 1.*(verb.* miynd*)* **to remember**. e.g. Ah cannut **mind** where ah put it = I don't recall the location where I placed that item.
>
> > *(I **mind**, you **mind**, he **minds**, not usually used in the past tense)*

moider

> 1.*(verb.* moydur*)* **pester**. e.g. Divn't **moider** yer old feller = Don't pester your father.

mott

1.*(noun.* mott*)* **girl**, or **woman**. e.g. **Mott**, you'll be a **mott** soon = Girl, you'll be a woman soon.

Pronounced moat, like boat, in West Cumbria.

mouncher

1.*(noun.* mownchur*)* **scrounger**, someone who is always in want of something from you for free such as cigarettes, money, your last dow of drink.

mowdy

1.*(noun.* maowdee*)* **mole**, the blind underground dwelling creature.

moy

1.*(noun.* moy*)* **mouth**. e.g. Shut yer **moy** = Please be quiet. (as seen on signs distributed around Cumbrian libraries).

Also sometimes used to describe the act of kissing.

mun

1.*(modal verb.* munn*)* **must**. e.g. Tha **mun** see yon = You must see that.

mush

1.*(noun.* mush*)* **face**, specifically **mouth**. e.g. Reet pal, do ya fancy a smack in the **mush** ? = Excuse me, would you like me to, perhaps, punch you generally in the face, but specifically in the area of your mouth? or Shut your **mush** = please be quiet.

Mutty Kitty

1.*(noun.* muttee kittee*)* A street game similar to leapfrog but played lined up against a brick wall. The object of the game being to see how many of your team can vault onto the other teams backs before their line collapses.

43

~N~

napper

> 1.*(noun.* napper*)* **head**. e.g. Gaffer's **Napper** = The Kings Head - a pub in Carlisle where you can always get a seat (or could until they refurbished it).

nash

> 1.*(verb.* nash*)* **to run**. e.g. If ya **nash**, y'll git yem quicker, like = If you should choose to run, it is likely that you will arrive at your dwelling place in less time.

> *(I **nash**, you **nash**, he **nashes**, she **nashes**, we **nash**, yous **nash**, they **nash**, I have **nashed**, I will **nash**, I am a **nasher**)*

> *See also **Knock-n-Nash**.*

neb

> 1.*(noun.* neb*)* **nose**. e.g. I cowped awer and bust me **neb** = I fell over and hurt my nose.

> *Note: Sometimes pronounced with a preceding 'sh' to make shneb.*

netty

> 1.*(noun.* nettee*)* **toilet**. e.g. He's well posh, he's got a **netty** indoors! = He must be rather affluent, he no longer has an outside lavatory.

nigh on

    1.*(adv.* niy on*)* **almost**, **nearly**. e.g. nigh on means **nigh on** the same as vanaye = nigh on means almost the same as vanaye.

    *See also **vanaye** and **vanya**.*

nix

    1.*(pronoun.* nicks*)* **nothing**. e.g. Am owing yer **nix** = I owe you nothing, oo-er, nothing at all.

    Pronounced nish in some areas.

nobbut knee high til a goose

    1.*(phrase.* nobbutt nee hiy till a goows*)* describes a **person of diminutive stature**. e.g. 'e wuz **nobbut knee high til a goose** = He was like a real person, only in miniature.

nowt

    1.*(pronoun.* nowt*)* **nothing**. e.g. Thuz **nowt** better'un lowpin' awer yats = There is nothing better than jumping over gates.

    *See also **owt**.*

~O~

oh five side / oh nine side

1.*(noun.* oh fiyv siyd / oh niyn siyd*)* geographic areas of the Morehouse Valley served by the '05' and 09' busses .

ower

Alternative spelling of awer.

owmun

1.*(phrase.* ahwmunn*)* **hey you**. e.g. **Owmun**, girroff yon! = Excuse me, would you mind getting off that.

owt

1.*(pronoun.* owt*)* **anything**. e.g. Av nivver sin **owt** like yon = Never have I seen anything such as that before.

oxter

1.*(noun.* okstur*)* **armpit**, **underarms**. e.g. 'is arl man picks 'im up be the **oxters** = His father elevates him by holding him under the arms.

~P~

pagga / pagger

    1.*(noun. paggur)* **fight**. e.g. You wanna **pagga**, pal? = Why sir, I challenge you to a duel!

    2.*(verb. paggur)* **to fight**.

paggered

    1.*(adj. paggurd)* **tired**, e.g. Am awer **paggered** to pagger. = I am too tired to fight.

pal

    1.*(noun. pal)* **person about to be clouted**. Not to be confused with marra, e.g. Watch it **pal** ! = You had better take care, person I am about to hit.

    Pal is a confusing word and can in fact be used as a friendly term with only the intonation differentiating hostility from friendship. If you are at all in doubt it is advisable to err on the side of caution, and take pal as being hostile.

parney

1.*(noun.* parnee*)* **water**. e.g. Ya divn't wanna lowp into yon **parney** = You don't want to jump into that water.

Probably from the Hindi word Pa-a-nee as Hindi was a common language in Burma (Myanmar) during British rule and may have been picked up during the war.

parrish

1.*(pronoun.* parrish*)* **area**. e.g. Are there any yats to lowp awer in this **parrish** ? = Are there any gates to jump over in this area?

peeve

1.*(noun.* peev*)* **alcoholic beverage**. e.g. 'Ave you got any **peeve**, I wanna git gattered = Do you have any alcohol, as I'd like to get a little drunk.

pen

1.*(noun.* pen*)* **hill**. Found in place names rather than used on its own. e.g. *Penrith* which may have its origins as Pen-rhudd (or similar) meaning Red Hill.

From the old Cumbric language.

potters fling

1.*(phrase.* potterz fling*)* To hold one nostril shut, then blow, ejecting mucus from other nostril.

Also known as farmer's hankey.

pun

1.*(noun.* pun*)* **pound sterling**. e.g. Can yer len us two **pun**? = Would you be so kind as to loan me two of your english pounds?

*See also **bar**.*

pure

1. *(adv, adj.* pyuwa*)* **very**. e.g. That's **pure** barrie that! = That is really rather good.

~Q~

queer'n

1.*(adv, adj.* kweerun*)* **very**. e.g. Thoos **queer'n** radge thoo, like = You are quite a character!

~R~

radge

1.*(adj.* radj*)* **bad** or **poor** or **not very good**. e.g. He's **radge** at lowpin awer yats = The standard of his gate jumping is not very high.

2.*(adj.* radj*)* **mad** or **angry**. e.g. the old gadgee went **radge** when he caught us playin' Hikey Dikey = The senior gentleman became a little agitated when he discovered us practicing our hurdling skills.

3.*(adj.* radj*)* **daft** or **crazy**. e.g. 'es a bit radge yon = That gentleman is somewhat unpredictable.

radgee

1.*(noun.* radjey*)* **person who is not very capable**. e.g. He's a bit of a **radgee** = He is a bit of a waste of skin/space.

2.*(noun.* radjee*)* **tantrum**. Radgees are generally 'taken'. e.g. He took a **radgee** when he caught them kids playing Hikey Dykey = When he found the children playing in his garden, he over reacted somewhat and started yelling and screaming, and ended up chasing them around the streets for over half an hour.

*See also **razzie**.*

razzie

1.*(noun.* razzee*)* **a hysteric anger fit**. e.g. He's having a **razzie** = He is a bit angry.

*See also **radgee**.*

ratch

1.*(verb.* ratsh*)* **to search, to hunt out.** e.g. He's on the **ratch** furra new bewer = He is looking for a new young lady to court.

*(I **ratch**, you **ratch**, he **ratches**, I **ratched**)*

See also scrat.

rive

1.*(verb.* riyv*)* **to pull.** e.g. Yerl **rive** it off if yer keep laikin wid it. = You'll pull it off if you keep playing with it.

*(I **rive**, you **rive**, he **rives**, I **rived**)*

rivin

1.*(adj.* riyvin*)* **hungry.** e.g. Aas **rivin**, can we gan git some scran? = I'm feeling rather pekish, shall we seek sustenance?

run

1.*(adv, preposition.* run*)* **around**. e.g. They talk funny **run** 'is way = They have a strange accent around his locality.

~S~

satched

1.*(adj.* satsht*)* **soaked**. e.g. It wuz cummin doon yal watter – I wuz **satched** = It rained rather hard and I received a thorough soaking.

scop

1.*(verb.* skop*)* **to throw**. e.g. Yon l'arl chore couldn't lowp awer yon yat, so I just **scopped** him awer = The young boy over there couldn't jump over that gate, so I threw him over.

*(I **scop**, you **scop**, he **scops**, I **scopped**)*

scordy

1.*(noun.* skordee*)* **tea** the drink. e.g. Mek us a cuppa **scordy** = Could you make me a cup of tea, please.

scrag end

1.*(noun.* skragg end*)* **the worst bit**. e.g. Ah only gut the **scrag end** = I only got the worst bit.

scran

1.*(noun.* skran*)* **food**, **meal**. e.g. Aas gan furra **scran** = I'm going to eat some food.

2.*(verb.* skran*)* **to eat**. e.g Yerl nivver **scran** arl yon = I'd suggest maybe your eyes are greedier than your stomach.

scrant

1.*(noun.* skrant*)* **hungry**. e.g. Aas gay **scrant** feller, should we gan scran? = I'm feeling rather peckish, shall we eat?

scrat

1.*(verb.* skratt*)* **search**. e.g. Ah wuz **scrattin** around fur ages fur me lowie after it fell outta me pocket when a lowped awer yon yat = I searched for a considerable time for my loose change after it spilled from my pockets as I vaulted over the gateway.

*(I **scrat**, you are **scratting**, he **scrats**, I **scratted**)*

2.*(noun.* skratt*)* **mess**. e.g. It wuz in a reet **scrat** = It was rather untidy.

screeve

1.*(noun.* skreev*)* **motor car**. e.g. What's yer **screeve** = What motor car are you currently driving?

scrow

1.*(noun.* skrow*)* **mess**. e.g. Git up yon stairs and tidy thas room, it's in a gay arl **scrow** = Would you mind going upstairs and tidying your bedroom please, it's rather messy.

scrunt

1.*(noun.* skrunt*)* **apple core**.

scud

1.*(verb.* skud*)* **beat**. e.g. Arl **scud** yer! = I will give you a thrashing!

54

scudding

1.*(noun.* skudding*)* **beating**. e.g. Is tha lookin' furra **scudding**, pal? = Are you looking for a fight?

sech / sec

1.*(determiner and pronoun.* sek*)* **such**. e.g. Tom Wrathall is **sech** a gran' fella = Tom Wrathall is such a nice man.

sen

1.*(noun.* sen*)* **self**. e.g. Watch the **sen** = Be careful.

shan

1.*(verb.* shan*)* **to embarrass**. e.g. Arl **shan** ya up if ye divn't lowp awer yonder yat! = I will embarrass you if you don't jump over that gate.

2.*(noun.* shan*)* **an embarrassment**. e.g. What a **shan**, eh! = That is such an embarrassment.

Shanks's pony

1.*(phrase.* shankseez pohwnee*)* **by foot**. e.g. Aas gan be **Shanks's pony** = I will be going by foot.

shant

1.*(adj.* shant*)* **embarassed**. e.g. I was dead **shant** when I cowped awer lowpin awer yonder yat = I was very embarrassed when I fell over jumping over that gate over there.

sin

1.*(verb.* sin*)* **seen**. e.g. 'Ave yer **sin** yon cowie? = Have you seen that thing?

skinches

1.*(noun.* skinshiz*)* **a declaration of immunity**. By declaring a state of skinches you cannot be given a Chinese burn, cannot have your hair pulled, and are generally immune from any torture or harassment. In Cumbria it is considered the most ill of manners to ignore skinches, and it is believed that in the past people would be banished from the county for transgressions of the immunity afforded by skinches. The word is simply uttered on its own. Sometimes accompanied by the display of crossed fingers. Skinches may be the most powerful defence known to man, and some believe it may be what protected OJ Simpson from prosecution.

shillies

1.*(noun.* shilleez*)* **decorative gravel**. e.g. Thaz gut **shillies** arl awer t'parish = You have made a mess with the gravel and spread it everywhere.

shlape

1.*(adj.* shlayp*)* **slippy.** e.g. Divn't lowp yon yat, the roads awer **shlape** on tother side and tha'll cowp awer. = I'd recommend not jumping that gate as the road on the other side is rather slippy and may result in a fall.

Very similar to the Old Norse and Icelandic sleip *which can also mean slippery in the sense of* crafty, cunning *or* tricksy.

shreddies

1.*(noun.* shreddeez*)* **underpants**.

*See also **grotts**.*

slatter

1.*(verb.* slattur*)* **to carelessly spill a liquid**. Whatcher dunt **slatter** yer soup arl down yer ganzee = Be careful that you don't spill your soup all down your jumper.

*(I **slatter**, you **slatter**, he **slatters**, I **slattered**)*

smart

1.*(adj.* smart*)* **good, good looking.** e.g. His bewer's well **smart**! = His girlfriend is really rather attractive.

sneck

    1.*(noun.* snek*)* **door latch**.

sneck lifter

    1.*(noun.* snek liftur*)* **your last sixpence**. This is what will allow you to 'lift the latch' of your local hostelry and buy your last pint in the hope of meeting friends who will buy you more. (Not quite) coincidentally, it is also the name of a local beer from the Cumbrian brewer Jennings.

sneck possett

    1.*(phrase.* snek possett*)* to not be invited or allowed into the house and left on the doorstep e.g. He wuz **sneck posset** = His wife was so upset that he didn't return from the local hostelry in time for his teas that she would not allow him back into the house and left him outside on the door step.

snib

    1.*(noun.* snib*)* **door lock/latch**. This is the little lock that can be used to keep a door unlocked. On a Yale type lock this is the little round lock button on the inside. The act of 'snibbing a door' is to engage the lock so that someone can enter without a key. The door is then said to be left 'on the **snib**'.

    2.*(verb.* snib*)* **to snib a door**. See above.

spawney

    1.*(adj.* spornee*)* **lucky**. e.g. He lowped awer the yat, but he was dead **spawny**, like = He jumped over the gate, but he only just made it!

    *See also **flukey** and **jousey**.*

spell

1.*(noun. spell)* **a break or rest from something**. e.g. Arm awer tired, as ganna have a **spell**, eh = I intend to take a short break from this activity that I am finding so tiring.

Also in use in Australia and New Zealand.

2.*(verb. spell)* **to give someone a break or rest from something**. e.g. Yer look tired, lad. Shift awer and arl **spell** yer = I shall give you a short break from your activities young man.

Also in use in Australia and New Zealand.

3.*(noun. spell)* **a splinter of wood**. e.g. Ah gut a **spell** in me 'and when ah lowped yon arl yat = I suffered getting a splinter in my hand from the degenerating wood of that old gate that I jumped.

spraff

1.*(verb. spraff)* **to steal**. e.g. Arm gonna **spraff** 'is lowie = I intend to steal that gentleman's money.

2.*(verb. spraff)* **tell tales on**, **grass up**. e.g. 'e **spraffed** on us for chorin' that gadgees cailo = He reported me to the authorities for procuring that gentleman's money by nefarious means.

*(I **spraff**, you **spraff**, he **spraffs**, I **spraffed**)*

spoggy

1.*(noun. spoggee)* **sparrow**. Passeroidea, Passeridae, genus Passer.

sploits

1.*(noun. splotyz)* **shoes**. e.g. His **sploits** gut arl clarty in the field. = His shoes got rather dirty in the field.

(Note: Sometimes prononced with an r rather than an l, giving 'sproits'.)

58

starving

    1.*(adj.* starving*)* **cold**. e.g. It's **starving** oot theyur. = It's a little chilly outside.

      Starving would normally refer to temperatures of below zero Celsius when it may be advisable to consider putting on clothing with long sleeves such as a long sleeved T-shirt.

starvation

    1.*(adj.* starvayshun*)* **very cold**. e.g. It's **starvation** oot theyur. = It really is rather chilly out today.

      Starvation would normally refer to temperatures of below minus 10 Celsius when one may wish to consider putting on a jumper if venturing outside for any extended period.

stotting

    1.*(verb.* stotting*)* **falling so hard that it bounces back up and splashes**. Specifically used with 'down' to describe very heavy rain. e.g. It's **stotting** down = It's raining rather heavily.

      *See also **yal watter**.*

strides

    1.*(noun.* striydz*)* **trousers**. e.g. Ah ripped me **strides** lowpin' awer yonder yat = I appear to have caused my trousers to be torn by jumping over the gate over there.

summat

    1.*(pronoun.* summert*)* **something**. e.g. There must be **summat** wrang, he can normally mek it awer yon yat easy = I think something is amiss as he is usually able to jump that gate with ease.

~T~

tapped

> 1.*(adj.* tapt*)* **stupid, mad, crazy.** e.g. Yoower **tapped** lad! = I think you are crazy, young fellow.

tapper / tappa

> 1.*(noun, offensive.* tappur*)* **one who is tapped.** e.g. He's a **tapper** = He is stupid / mad / crazy.
>
> > *Not the most politically correct of phrases, but coming literally from the tapping of the finger to the temple indicating that someone has problems in the head. Hence a 'tappa's bar' in Cumbria may not be the place to purchase Spanish snacks.*
>
> 2.*(noun.* tappur*)* **scrounger.** Someone who is always in want of something from you for free such as cigarettes, money, your last dow of drink.

tarn

> 1.*(noun.* tahrn*)* **a small lake**. Often, but not always, in a mountain setting.
>
> > *From the Old Norse* tjörn *meaning pond.*

taytee

> 1.*(noun.* tay-tee*)* **potatoe**. e.g. Yur cannot mek a **taytee** pot if thee 'asn't gut any **tayee** = Potatoes are a key ingredient in Potatoe-pot.

taytee ed

> 1.*(noun.* tay-tee-ed*)* **daft person**. e.g. Oi, **taytee ed** = Hello, daft person.

telt

> 1.*(pt verb.* telt*)* **told**. e.g. Arv **telt** yer aready! = I believe you are asking me to repeat myself.

tethera

1.*(cardinal number.* tethurra*)* **three**. The third number. Part of the old Cumbrian sheep counting scheme.

See phrase book.

thoo

1.*(pronoun.* thoow*)* **you**. e.g. **Thoo**'s lookin like thas bin in a pagga = You look like you got caught up in some fisticuffs.

Also notice the use of 'thas' (pronounced thaz) which is an irregular past tense of thoo's being a combination and contraction of 'thoo has'.

thon

1.*(pronoun.* thon*)* **that person**, **him**, **her**. e.g. Deeks **thon**, thurra reet state = Would you look at him/her, they are not exactly looking their best.

thrang

1.*(adj.* thrang*)* **busy.** e.g. Ist thee gay **thrang**? = Are you very busy?

tidy

1.*(adj.* tydee*)* **good**, **acceptable**, **decent**. e.g. Yer quite **tidy** when yerv gut yer clart on. = Baby, you look wonderful tonight.

to-do

1.*(noun.* terdoo*)* **outrage**, **uproar.** e.g. A reet **to-do** aboot nowt = Much ado about nothing.

tother

1.*(adj, pronoun.* tuthur*)* **the other**. e.g. It gans in yan ear an straight oot **tother**. = He's not the best listener.

touched

1.*(adj.* tutsht*)* See tapped.

traipse

1.*(verb.* trayps*)* **wander aimlessly or seemingly without purpose**. e.g 'e **traipses** run yon fields fur oors = He wanders around those fields for hours.

*(I **traipse**, you **traipse**, he **traipses**, I **traipsed**, you are **traipsing**, they are **traipsers**)*

troff

1.*(noun.* troff*)* See scran.

tunch

1.*(noun.* tunsh*)* **turnip**.

tup

1.*(noun.* tup*)* **uncastrated ram**.

2.*(verb. vulg.* tup*)* **to copulate**.

3.*(noun. vulg.* tup*)* **an act of copulation**.

twine

1.*(verb.* twiyn*)* **to moan** or **whinge**. e.g. Quit **twinin'** just coz the gadgee caught yer lowpin 'is dyke. = Stop moaning just because the man caught you playing hikey dikey.

*(I **twine**, you **twine**, he **twines**, I **twined**, you are **twining**, they are **twiners**)*

tyan / tan

1. *(cardinal number.* tyan*)* **two**. The second number. Part of the old Cumbrian sheep counting scheme.

See phrase book.

~U~

up street

>   1.*(noun.* up streeyt*)* **town** or **shopping area**. e.g. As gan **up street** fur shopping = I am going into the town for my shopping.

us

>   1.*(pronoun.* uz*)* **me**. The first person singular. e.g. Giv **us** yan o them = Would you be so kind as to give me one of those.

~V~

vanaye

1.*(adv.* van-iy*)* **almost**. e.g. He **vanaye** med it awer yon yat = That gentlemen very nearly made it over that gate over there.

*See also **nigh on** and **vanya**.*

vanya

1.*(adv.* vanyah*)* **almost**. e.g. It's **vanya** time ter gan yam = It's almost time to be heading off home.

*See also **nigh on** and **vanaye**.*

~W~

waffey

> 1.*(adj.* waffeey*)* **unsteady**. e.g. Ah felt arl **waffey** after ah got 'it by yon coddie. = I became rather unsteady on my feet after the mishap with the pebble.

watter

> 1.*(noun.* wattur*)* **water**. Two parts hydrogen to one part oxygen.

waz

> 1.*(noun.* waz*)* **wee-wee**. e.g. As gan furra **waz** = I'm off to empty the old bladder.
>
> *See also **lag**.*

weez

> 1.*(phrase.* weez*)* **Who is?** e.g. **Weez** yon old gadgee, eh ? = Do you happen to know the identity of the male senior citizen over there ?

weezaw

> 1.*(phrase.* weez-orr*)* **Who are?**, e.g. **Weezaw** that, eh? = Do you happen to know the identity of all those people?
>
> 2.*(possessive determiner.* weez-orr*)* **whose?**, e.g. **Weezaw** yon kady? = To whom does that hat belong?

welt

> 1.*(verb.* welt*)* **hit**. e.g. I had to **welt** him cuz he tried to shan uz up, like. = He tried to embarass me, so I hit him (your honour).
>
> *(I **welt**, you **welt**, he **welts**, I **welted**, your are **welting**, they are **welters**)*

wisht

1.*(verb.* wish-t*)* **be quiet**. e.g. **Wisht** yersel, pal = Please be quite, sir.

~Y~

yacker

> 1.*(noun.* yackur*)* **farm worker**. e.g. **Yackers** are better it lowpin yats thun townies, eh = I believe farm workers to be better at jumping gates than those who live in the urbanised areas.

yal watter

> 1.*(phrase.* yahl wattur*)* **heavy rain**. e.g. As nut gan yat lowpin the day, it's comin' doon **yal watter** oot theeyur = I shall postpone my gate jumping excursion as it's raining rather too heavy outdoors today.

yam

> 1.*(noun.* yam*)* **home**. A person's dwelling place. e.g. As gam **yam** = I shall be returning home.

> *Sometimes spelled **yem**.*

yan

> 1.*(cardinal number.* yan*)* **one**. The first number. Comes right after none, and directly before two or tyan. e.g. Giz **yan** uh them = Could I have one of those, please.
>
> > *See phrase book.*

yance

> 1.*(adv.* yans*)* **once**. e.g. If arv telt yer **yance** I've telt yer a dozen times = If I have told you once I have told you a dozen times.

yat

> 1.*(noun.* yat*)* **gate**. e.g. Lowp awer t'**yat** = Jump over the gate.
>
> 2.*(phrase.* yat*)* **are you at?**. e.g. Where's **yat**? = Where are you?

yat stoop

> 1.*(noun.* yat stoop*)* **gatepost**. e.g. Yon yat's 'angin off **yat stoop** = That gate is in need of repair.

yatter

> 1.*(verb.* yattur*)* **to talk**. e.g. What yer **yatterin'** about? = What are you talking about?
>
> > *(I **yatter**, you **yatter**, he **yatters**, I **yattered**, you are **yattering**, they are **yatterers**)*

yawwa

> 1.*(phrase.* yawwah*)* **Could you repeat that?**, e.g. **Yawwa**? = I'm sorry, I didn't quite catch that. Could you possibly repeat it for me?
>
> 2.*(phrase.* yawwah*)* **I don't believe you**. e.g. **Yawwa**?! = I don't believe you, what are you talking about, don't talk daft, lad.

yem

    1.*(noun.* yem*)* **home**. A person's dwelling place.

> *Often spelled and pronounced* yam*, but* yem *sounds much better in sentences such as "Git the sen **yem** quick, lad, it'll be coming doon yal watter in nee time = hurry on home as it looks like rain."*

yon

    1.*(pronoun and determiner.* yon*)* **that**. e.g. Divn't lowp awer **yon** yat = Don't jump over that gate.

yonder

    1.*(pronoun.* yondur*)* **that.** Variant of yon, specifically more distant. e.g. Divn't lowp awer **yonder** yat = Don't jump over that gate over there.

~Z~

zoff

1. *(adj.* zoff*)* **he / she / it is off**. Used during the calling of the register in school classrooms to indicate that a fellow pupil is absent but can also be used more generally. e.g. See yon cheese ? **Zoff** ! = Do you see that cheese, it is past its prime and has entered its rancid stage.

Cumbrian Phrase Book

Greetings and platitudes

Hello (formal)
Arlreet

Hello (informal)
Arlreet marra

Hello (casual)
Owdo

Good morning
Arlreet

Goodbye
See yer

How are you?
Arlreet?

Owz ya fettle?

What news do you have?
What's the crack?

..., please
..., eh

Thank you
Ta

That's enough, thank you.
Nee mare, ta.

Numbers

The following is the old Cumbrian counting scheme. It was widely used for the counting of sheep, and only *yan* is in general use today.

Yan	=	One (1)
Tyan	=	Two (2)
Tethera	=	Three (3)
Methera	=	Four (4)
Pimp	=	Five (5)
Sethera	=	Six (6)
Lethera	=	Seven (7)
Hovera	=	Eight (8)
Dovera	=	Nine (9)
Dick	=	Ten (10)
Bumfit	=	Fifteen (15)
Giggot	=	Twenty (20)

The counting method is actually not strictly decimal, however. The numbers 1 to 10 were counted as normal, but 11 to 14 would be counted as "1 and 10" etc. 16 to 19 would be "1 and 15" and so on. The multiples of 5 having their own word.

It should also be noted that there are numerous variations to be found in Cumbrian numbering depending on where in Cumbria you are and who you speak to.

Having been handed down verbally, spellings can also be contentious.

74

Getting around

Can you tell me how to get to ... ?
Where's ... at?

Follow this road
Gan doon 'ere

... until you get to ...
... till the gets ter yon ...

I'm going that way, I'll show you.
Away, as gan that way anor'.

It's just past the bridge.
It's just past yon bridge.

I'm lost
Ah divn't know where am at, eh.

Are you on foot or in a car?
Yer gan be Shanks's or yer gorra screeve?

A single ticket to ..., please.
A ticket ter gan ter ..., ta.

A return ticket to ..., please.
A ticket to gan an' git yam fer ..., ta.

Hotels

I would like a single room, please.
Ave yer gorra room? Jus' fer mesell, like?

Is breakfast included?
Der yer dee a brekky anorl? Does it cost owt?

What time is breakfast served?
Willafta girrup early furrus scran tomorrer?

What time is check out?
When av a gorra gan?

I have lost my room key.
Ah dunno where me keys at, eh. Can yer lerruz back in?

 75

Restaurants

A table for four
Yer gorra chebble fur us fower?

> *(Note, unless your group includes a number of sheep regular English numbers should be used rather than the Cumbrian numbering system. Use of the latter in this kind of situation will just make you look daft.)*

I made a reservation
A phoned yuz afore.

Two cups of tea, please.
A coupla cups a scordy, eh.

Could you tell me where the toilets (restrooms) are please?
Wherez the bogs at, eh?

Discussing The Weather

It's raining quite heavily again
'Ts comin' doon yal watter, eh

This rain is quite heavy
'Ts stottin doon

It's rather wet today
'Ts gay wet, like eh.

I see the sun has come out again
Whit's yon gert glishy ball o'fire in the sky.. run, run fer yer lives. Git the sen indoors quick, like. It's nut reet, that.

Getting out of trouble

Please leave me alone.
Away chess with yer.

I am not from around here.
As not fre run 'ere.

Could someone please call the police?
Git the 'orneys, eh!

This fellow looks like he needs an ambulance.
Lerrim alone, he'll be areet in a bit.

Discussing your visit to Cumbria when you get home

It was a very enjoyable holiday
Was grand, eh. Loved it. Spot on, like. Yer should gan yersells, it's barie.

Pronunciation of Some Cumbrian Place Names

Aspatria: Spya-tree

Barrow-in-Furness: Barruh in Furnuss

Brougham: Bruhm

Broughton: Brortun

Burgh By Sands: Bruff by Sandz

Carlisle: Car-liyul

Distington: Dissintun

Houghton: Howtun

Keswick: Kezzik

Raughton Head: Rafton Hed

Torpenhow*: Truppenuh

Whitehaven: White 'evvun

Workington: Wuckin'tun

> *Torpenhow is a triple tautology being the combination of three words meaning hill. Tor, Pen and How. Thus making Torpenhow Hill, to the South-South-East of Torpenhow itself (54.74028, -3.2348) a quadruple tautology - literally translating as Hill-hill-hill Hill.

What If They'd Been Cumbrian

Ever wondered what it would have been like if Churchill, Lincoln and Lennon were Cumbrian? Read on...

We'll gan on till the finish, we'll pagga in France, well give 'em a batterin on the sea and other parnee, we'll keep paggerin and gittin dead radge, we'll defend us parrish whativver it costs us, we'll belt 'em in Silloth, we'll scud 'em at Allonby, we'll batter 'em in the fields and up street, we'll fight up fells; we'll nivver give over, eh.

Winston Churchill

It's yan la'l step furra gadgee, yan gert lowp fur fwolk.

Neil Armstrong

At the start the gaffer med the 'even an' the grun. The grun wuz a bit of a nowt and it wuz arl dark and that, eh. An' the Spirit of the arl gadgee wuz 'ovverin awer the fyace o the parney.

Genesis 1.1-2

Arv gut a dream the day.
Arv gut a dream that yan day ivry dale'll be cheered, ivry crag and ivry fell'll be med low, the rough spots'll be med smoother, the bent bits'll git straightened, we'll see how barey the gaffer is an all folks'll see it together.

Martin Luther King, August 1963

We wanna gan ter the moon. We wanna gan ter the moon in nee mare than ten yeayers and that, nut coz it's easy or owt, but coz it's a bit 'ard, coz it'll mek us better at stuff, an coz it's summat we'd be fairly 'appy ter dee, summat we're nut gonna purroff, summat we're gonna win and all that.

John F Kennedy, September 1962

Eighty seven yeayers ago oor arl fellers med a new nation on this big old island, med free like, and so that arl gadgees is the same, eh.

Abraham Lincoln, November 1863

Ter them that's waitin fur what they sez on the wireless, the U-turn, arv only gut yan thing ter tell: Thee can turn if ther fancies. This lasso's nut ganna.

Margaret Thatcher, October 1980

*Arl the world's a stage, eh
An' arl the gadgees and lassos merely players:
They 'ave thur gan oots and thur comins in;
An' yan gadgee in 'is time laiks loadsa parts,
'is acts bein' seven ages. At fust the bairden,
Twinin' an' bowkin' in the nurse's arms.
An' then the radgee la'l chore, wid 'is satchel*

William Shakespeare, from As You Like It

Lerrum scran Kendal Mint Cake.

Not Marie Antoinette!

Famous Texts

If thee can keep yer bonce while rest of 'em
Are losin' theeyurs an sayin' it's yoower fault,
If thee can trust yersen when ivryone thinks yer tellin lies,
But nut be arrished by them thinkin' it;
If you can dee summat fur that minute
When you've nashed fur a minute,
Yoowers is the Earth and all its stuff,
And – tek heed – yer'll be gadgee, la'l feller!

Rudyard Kipling, If

An did them sploits a lang while back
Walk upon them fells and that?

William Blake, Jerusalem

'magine thuz nee 'evven
Snorrard if yer givirra gan
Nee 'ell doon theeyur
Up theeyur only sky
'magine arl the fwolk livin' fur terday

'magine thuz nee countries, eh
Snorrard ter dee
Nowt ter kill or die fur
Nee god crack neethur
'magine arl the fwolk livin' life in peace

John Lennon, Imagine

Appendices

Look North

Throughout my life I have been constantly frustrated by a tendency throughout the world to believe that England stops when you get to Manchester or Liverpool.

While Northumbria in the north east is well known as land of the Geordies it seems to exist in some bizarre nowhere land – if England ends around the M62 then just where does Northumbria fit in to the jigsaw?

For almost 150 miles to the north of Manchester and Liverpool – cities whose attitudes are widely considered to be the definition of northerness – there is a black hole in the collective consciousness of many when it comes to that great tract of land to the west, between Lancashire and Scotland.

If the north west of England stops not far north of the East Lancs Road and the Manchester Ship canal, then what on earth is the green and pleasant land that you drive through before crossing the border.

That'll be Cumbria, along with Northumbria, the true north of England and whose people are the rightful claimant to the moniker 'Northerners'.

But this appendix is not about ranting. Rather it is a mathematical and scientific proof of the geographic facts of the north.

What is presented over the next couple of pages can be used to irrefutably demonstrate that Cumbrians (and

Northumbrians) are the true Northerners A few miles further north and the Cumbrian menfolk may be tempted to put on a tribal wooly skirt whenever occasion allows temptation to get the better of them. A few miles further south and you may as well call a Cumbrian a Midlander.

This is not baseless conjecture. It is fact. And over the next couple of pages you'll see the proof.

Step 1 – This is England

Let us first consider where England sits and its orientation.

England is shown here in black against the rest of the mainland UK and Ireland. If you didn't know that then I guess you just found this book in a bin or something.

Step 2 – The Rule of Thirds

If we are to consider England as consisting of The North, The Midlands and The South then we must divide the landmass equally into thirds. To be consistent we should also divide the country into three from West to East.

This can be achieved by creating a 3x3 grid consisting of North, South, East, West, North-West, North-East, South-East, South-West and The Midlands.

NW	N	NE
W	Midlands	E
SW	S	SE

Step 3 –Circle Squared

A circle is the smallest North-South-East-West symmetrical shape which can enclose the whole of England, so we map our 3x3 grid into a circle using 45° segments centered around the cardinal points.

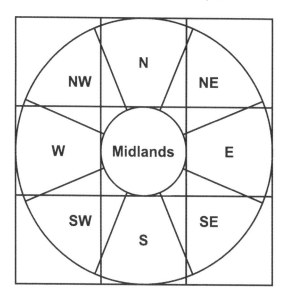

Step 4 – Circle Squared

We then remove the square grid leaving us with a circle divided into equal sections of north-south and east-west distance.

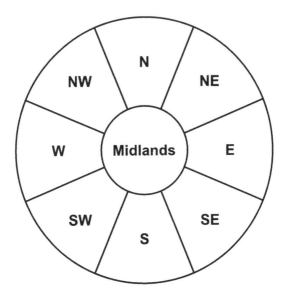

Each cardinal section above is exactly one third of the whole in its own direction. i.e. North, Midlands and South are each one third vertically. West, Midlands and East are exactly one third of the whole horizontally.

Step 5 – Overlay the Compass

We then scale and overlay this divided compass, aligned with north, on our outline of England.

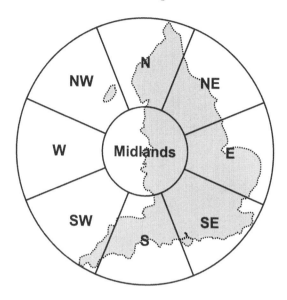

This is the smallest circle that can contain the whole of the English mainland.

If you have any knowledge of the geography of England you may have already spotted some of the surprises over the page.

Step 6 – Adding some names

If we add the names of some well-known towns and cities...

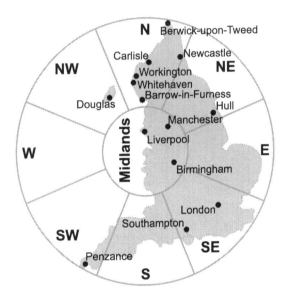

You can see that Liverpool and Manchester undeniably join Birmingham in the Midlands. Newcastle is actually in the North, not the North East and the only place in England that can truly claim to be in the North West is the Isle of Man!

Lancaster is pretty much on the North/Midlands border meaning that The north of England consists almost entirely of Cumbria and Northumbria. Anyone else who claims to be a northerner is just fantasizing.

And if you are still reading at this point I'd like to be cheeky and ask for support for a couple of good causes.

First of all, GonMad/No Original Thought's own **BlueBadgeParking.com**. This website provides a free, online, crowd-sourced database and map of disabled parking spaces all over the world.

BlueBadgeParking.com relies on people like you updating the database with parking spaces that you know about.

The maps can be printed or the whole database can be loaded into a SatNav (most makes supported) to lead disabled people directly to the closest space.

Also, you may not be aware of a disease which affects more people the higher the latitude in which they live - **i.e. it's a disease which affects more people depending on how much of a Northerner they are**.

This disease is *Multiple Sclerosis*. There is no cure and its cause is unknown – also why it seems more prevalent the further north you go (or south in the southern hemisphere) is unknown.

The disease affects about twice as many women as it does men, and is usually diagnosed in the twenties or thirties.

It is an evil disease that affects every sufferer in a different way but can cause blindness, make walking impossible, affect talking, eating, breathing, hand function, cognition... you name it, anything that you do can be badly affected by MS.

The disease attacks the brain and spinal cord and can lead to progressive disability which accumulates over time. There is no predicting the long term path of the disease or even knowing day to day how bad you will be.

If you are looking for a charity to support there are three that don't get the attention they deserve. They work in different ways, some supporting research, some supporting sufferers and their families and providing the newly diagnosed with invaluable information.

I am in no way associated with these charities, but they all do great work in their different ways and are very close to me and my partner.

So, next time you're thinking of raising money for a worthy cause please consider:

The MS Society: http://www.mssociety.org.uk/

The MS Resource Centre: http://www.msrc.co.uk/

The MS Trust: www.mstrust: http://www.mstrust.org.uk

The only lake…

If you are still wondering which body of water is technically the only lake in the Lake District it's Bassenthwaite Lake.

~

Now... away chess yersel' an' dee summat worthwhile.

Just keep yersel' in good fettle.

10175422R00068

Printed in Germany
by Amazon Distribution
GmbH, Leipzig